SOUTH EAST ASIA
RAILWAYS

PETER J. GREEN

AMBERLEY

Acknowledgements

I would like to say thank you to James Waite for permitting me to use a number of his photographs in this book. These have helped to fill some of the gaps in my own collection. James has also helped with information for various captions.

My thanks are also due to Val Brown for her assistance with checking my text for errors.

First published 2022

Amberley Publishing
The Hill, Stroud
Gloucestershire, GL5 4EP

www.amberley-books.com

Copyright © Peter J. Green, 2022

The right of Peter J. Green to be identified as the Author of this work has been asserted in accordance with the Copyrights, Designs and Patents Act 1988.

ISBN 978 1 4456 9888 5 (print)
ISBN 978 1 4456 9889 2 (ebook)

British Library Cataloguing in Publication Data.
A catalogue record for this book is available from the British Library.

Typesetting by SJmagic DESIGN SERVICES, India.
Printed in Great Britain.

Contents

Introduction

South East Asia, with its metre gauge railways, is a popular destination for railway enthusiasts from all over the world. Here, we look at the national railways of Thailand, Myanmar, Malaysia, Cambodia, and Vietnam in the twenty-first century. While these railways are modernising at varying rates, it is still possible to step back into the past and experience train travel behind diesel traction, often in carriages with windows that open, through varied and interesting landscapes. The railways of all these countries are attractive in various ways. Semaphore signalling is disappearing rapidly but can still be seen in parts of Thailand, Myanmar, Malaysia, and Vietnam. A visit to Myanmar to experience train travel there is highly recommended. The suburban railways around Yangon (previously Rangoon), particularly the circular railway, are something that should not be missed. Travelling on the old Burma Railway over the River Kwai Bridge in Thailand is also an interesting and enjoyable experience. In Malaysia, the Jungle Line offers a taste of how things used to be, while Cambodia and Vietnam also offer journeys to attractive destinations behind their diesel-powered trains.

The State Railway of Thailand (SRT) was founded in 1890 as the Royal State Railways of Siam, the name changing in 1951. The Northern Line was originally built to standard gauge, but was converted to metre gauge by 1929, to conform to the rest of the system. Currently, SRT has over 4,000 km of track, most of it single-track railway with passing loops, although there is some double track around Bangkok.

Myanmar was previously known as Burma. Railway operation began in 1877, and in 1896 the various railway lines were amalgamated to form the Burma Railway Company. In 1928, it became Burma Railways, the name changing to Myanma Railways (or Myanmar Railways in English) in 1989. Currently, Myanmar's metre gauge railway system is over 11,000 km in length. Most of the system is single track with passing loops, but the routes from Yangon to Mandalay and Pyay are largely double track. Yangon's busy circular railway, part of the suburban network, is almost 46 km long with thirty-nine stations. Railway lines are still being built in Myanmar and four new lines are currently under construction. British-built signalling can be seen in many places around the country.

In Malaysia, the metre gauge railway operations are in Peninsular Malaysia and Sabah in northern Borneo.

Keretapi Tanah Melayu Berhard (KTM), or Malayan Railways Limited, is the main railway operator in Peninsular Malaysia. The system consists of the West Coast and East Coast Lines and a number of branches, the total length being 1,699 km. Most of the railway is single track, but electrification and conversion to double track is progressing. Construction of the first railway, for agricultural development, commenced around 1869, between Johor Bahru and Gunong Pulai. Construction of metre gauge railways for the transport of tin began in 1882.

The Sabah State Railway (SSR), previously known as the North Borneo Railway, is a 134-km line from Tanjung Aru, Kota Kinabalu, to Tenom in the Interior Division. Originally intended mainly to transport tobacco to the coast, construction of the railway started in 1896.

Vietnam Railways (Duong sat Viet Nam) operates the railway system in Vietnam. The 1,600-km metre gauge main line runs from Hanoi to Ho Chi Minh City (Saigon), with branches off the main line, as well as from Hanoi. The single-track main line was constructed in the 1880s under French colonial rule. There is also a standard gauge line from Hanoi to China, and some sections of dual gauge track.

Cambodia's first railway was opened in stages, between 1932 and 1940, from Phnom Penh to Poipet on the Thailand border. The metre gauge railway was 387 km long. A second line, 264 km long, to Sihanoukville was opened progressively between 1960 and 1969. With track and equipment badly run down following the Cambodian Civil War, all railway operations ceased by 2009. From 2010, the railway was slowly rebuilt, first under Toll Royal Railway and then Royal Railway after the Toll Group withdrew. The line through to Sihanoukville reopened for freight services in 2012, and for passengers in 2016. The line to Poipet was reopened by 2018, and it was expected that the cross-border connection to Thailand would reopen in 2020, but it has been delayed by the Covid pandemic. A passenger service between Phnom Penh and its international airport commenced in 2018, using a new, short branch line from the Sihanoukville line.

Photographing railways has been my major interest for many years, a hobby that has taken me all round the world. My first visit to South East Asia was in 2002, when I visited Singapore, Malaysia and Thailand, before flying home via Hong Kong. I was able to experience something of the railways in each of these countries, spending time around Singapore station before taking the train to Malaysia, where I visited Sentul Works, near Kuala Lumpur. In Thailand, I explored the railways around Bangkok and travelled along the old Burma Railway to the River Kwai Bridge and beyond. Since then, I have visited the region every year to photograph the railways. My first visit to Vietnam was from the end of December 2005 until early January 2006 and is memorable for the heavy rain that fell every day until the day I was flying out! Nevertheless, I managed to take some photographs at Da Nang on that last day, one of which is included here. Cambodia was visited twice in 2006. Each time I went round the locomotive depot, but there was little railway activity then. For various reasons, I did not visit Myanmar until much later. My experiences there have been very good and, despite the rapid modernisation, it is, for me, currently one of the most interesting countries in South East Asia. It is definitely my intention to continue to visit the railways of South East Asia for some years to come!

Thailand

The principal station and the headquarters of the State Railway of Thailand (SRT) are located at Hualampong, Bangkok. Opened in 1916, the station has twelve platforms from which trains run to all parts of Thailand. Here, Hitachi Co-Co diesel-electric locomotive No. 4519 waits for departure time with train 169, the 15.35 to Yala in southern Thailand. Alsthom No. 4218 is alongside with the 15.20 to Ubon Ratchathani. 1 July 2018.

Alsthom No. 4413 arrives at Bangkok station, at Hualampong, with train 202, the 06.05 from Phitsanulok in northern Thailand. The maintenance facility for diesel multiple units (DMUs) is on the left, with a General Electric (GE) diesel outside, and the power box is on the right. Thailand's Alsthom Co-Co diesel-electric locomotives, model AD24C, were built in four batches (SRT types ALS, AHK, ALD and ADD) between 1974 and 1985. They were fitted with Pielstick engines of 2,250 to 2,400 hp. A total of 113 were built by Alsthom, Henschel & Krupp. 15 February 2019.

Alsthom No. 4413 passes the carriage sidings as it heads train 201, the 09.25 to Phitsanulok, away from Bangkok station. One of the station pilots, a GE diesel, is on the left. 6 May 2014.

Hitachi No. 4510 has just crossed the Saen Saeb Canal and is approaching Yommarat as it heads the 09.25 to Phitsanulok away from Bangkok. The grey, red and pink livery carried by a number of these locomotives was designed to match the silver-grey of SRT's new Chinese-built sleeping coaches. Twenty-two of these Co-Co diesel-electric locomotives, model 8FA-36C, were built by Hitachi in 1993. They are fitted with twin Cummins engines producing a total of 2,860 hp and are SRT type HID. 22 May 2019.

The Eastern Line leaves the main line to the north at Yommarat. A few kilometres along the Eastern Line is Makkasan station, where the SRT's principal railway works is located. The elevated, standard gauge, Airport Link railway from Suvarnabhumi Airport to the city is on the right, with the railway works behind. On the left, a Tokyu DMU departs as train 388, the 07.05 Chachoengsao to Bangkok, while a second Tokyu DMU forming train 281, the 08.00 Bangkok to Kabin Buri, waits in the station. 5 November 2015.

With the elevated line from Suvarnabhumi Airport on the left, No. 4004 heads a container train, from Lat Krabang Inland Container Terminal to Bang Sue yard, through Asok station in Bangkok. GE supplied fifty of these Co-Co diesel-electric locomotives to SRT between 1963 and 1965. They are model UM12C Shovel Nose, SRT type GE. A second member of the class is at the back of the train. 9 February 2018.

The freight-only railway line to Klong Toey yard and Bangkok Port diverges from the Eastern Line at Makkasan. On most weekdays, a container train runs from the yard to the port. The train is seen here passing the road entrance to the port on At Narong Road with GE No. 4024 in charge. The containers will be unloaded through a gate in the wall around the port, located a little farther on. 8 December 2014.

Hitachi Co-Co diesel-electric No. 4514 crosses the Samsen Canal as it approaches Samsen station with an empty stock train from Bangkok to Bang Sue. The train is formed of sleeping cars, built in China, which will be cleaned and serviced at Bang Sue carriage sidings. It will be returned to Bangkok later in the day, in time for its next overnight working. 23 April 2017.

Sprinter No. 2512, forming a Bang Son to Bang Sue shuttle service, is pictured arriving at Bang Sue station, 8 km north of Bangkok. Thailand's principal diesel depot, a freight yard, and carriage sidings are located at Bang Sue. The Southern Line diverges to the north of the station. A new station is currently being built next to the old one and will become Bangkok's main station. The sprinter was built by British Rail Engineering Limited (BREL) and is similar to a British Class 158. 24 April 2017.

Thonburi station was the original Bangkok terminus of the main line to the south of Thailand, but is now at the end of a 5-km branch line off the Southern Line from Bangkok station. The original Thonburi station is closed and the old station building is incorporated into Siriraj Hospital. The present-day Thonburi station was previously known as Bangkok Noi and is located next to the locomotive depot, about 1 km west of the original station. Here, various diesel locomotives and DMUs can be seen on the depot, as well as two Japanese Pacifics. 7 December 2013.

Japanese Pacifics Nos 850 and 824 stand outside the shed at Thonburi. Both were built by Nippon Sharyo, in 1950 and 1949 respectively. They are part of SRT's working steam fleet and are used on around four special trains each year. On the left is Henschel 0-6-0 diesel-hydraulic shunter No. 75, SRT type HAS, built in 1986. 20 February 2016.

Krupp B-B diesel-hydraulic No. 3121 approaches Thonburi station with train 252, the 04.50 Prachuap Khiri Khan to Thonburi. Twenty-seven of these 1,500-hp locomotives, model DH1500BB, were built in 1969. None of these locomotives were active at the time of writing. 24 December 2006.

Train 259, the 13.55 Thonburi to Nam Tok, arrives at Charan Sanitwong, about 1 km from Thonburi, behind GE No. 4042. Note the semaphore signal with a fixed distant arm. Construction of a section of the Sky Train urban railway is proceeding in the background. 19 February 2016.

Bang Pa-in is situated around 60 km north of Bangkok. Here, Alsthom No. 4129 approaches the station with train 111, the 07.00 Bangkok to Den Chai. Bang Pa-In is the location of the Royal Summer Palace of Thailand. 2 July 2014.

Alsthom No. 4222 powers an oil tank train, bound for Phitsanulok, through Ayutthaya station. Note the school children playing football on the platform by the old water crane. Ayutthaya is a former capital of Thailand, 85 km north of Bangkok. 12 July 2013.

The Northern and North Eastern Lines diverge at Ban Phachi Junction, 18 km north of Ayutthaya. Alsthom No. 4219 heads an oil tank train from the Northern Line into the yard. Here, the locomotive will run round its train before heading along the North Eastern Line to Ban Pok Pek oil terminal. 4 July 2018.

Daewoo DMU, forming train 7, the 08.30 special express from Bangkok to Chiang Mai, departs from Lop Buri. Note the monkey statue on the platform. The city is noted for the many monkeys that live in the ruined temples around the station. 12 December 2018.

Alsthom No. 4415 arrives at Lop Buri with train 112, the 07.30 Den Chai to Bangkok. The remains of a ruined temple are on the right. 11 December 2018.

Two old cranes, both built by Thomas Smith & Sons (Rodley), near Leeds, are displayed next to the old locomotive depot at Pak Nam Pho. 25-ton steam crane No. 24, built in 1930, is at the front. 12-ton hand crane No. 11, built in 1923, is behind. Pak Nam Pho is approximately 250 km north of Bangkok. 6 July 2015.

Co-Co diesel-electric No. 70104 waits at Phitsanulok with an empty cement train, bound for Hin Lap cement works. The locomotive is one of twelve owned by TPI Polene PLC for hauling their trains to cement terminals throughout Thailand. Built by CSR Zhiyang, China, they are fitted with Caterpillar 3516B HD engines of 2,760 hp. 4 December 2017.

Two versions of the Davenport diesel-electric locomotive were supplied to SRT. The Bo-Bo single cab type was introduced in 1952, and the double-ended Co-Co version in 1955. Both types were fitted with Caterpillar D397 engines of 500 hp, one in the single cab version and two in the double-ended type. Here, Bo-Bo No. 527 shunts the yard at Sila-At, 487 km north of Bangkok. This locomotive is now stored at Makkasan Works, Bangkok. 15 June 2009.

Hitachi No. 4503 shunts sleeping cars at Chiang Mai. These coaches will form train 10, the 18.00 to Bangkok, due to arrive at 06.50 the next day. Chiang Mai is the terminus of the Northern Line, 751 km from Bangkok. 9 December 2017.

Alsthom No. 4102 runs through Saraburi, 113 km from Bangkok on the North Eastern Line, with a train of empty oil tanks from Ubon Ratchathani to Ban Pok Pek oil terminal. The blue stripe carried by the locomotive indicates that it has been rebuilt with an MTU engine. 16 December 2017.

At Kaeng Khoi Junction, the direct line to Nong Khai and the freight line to Chachoengsao via Khlong Sip Kao Junction, diverge from the Bangkok to Ubon Ratchathani line. Qishuyan SDA3 No. 5120 arrives with a container train bound for Laem Chabang Port, via Chachoengsao. Twenty of these 3,190 hp Co-Co diesel-electric locomotives were supplied to SRT between 2013 and 2015. 17 December 2018.

Zhiyang No. 70106 heads an empty cement train to Hin Lap, away from Kaeng Khoi Junction. The train is made up of cement tanks and containers for bagged cement. 27 March 2019.

A lineup of motive power stands outside the shed at Kaeng Khoi locomotive depot. The locomotives are, from left to right, Alsthom AHK No. 4217, Hitachi HID No. 4520 and GE GEA No. 4533, with a second GEA behind. Thirty-eight of these GEA Co-Co diesel-electric locomotives, fitted with twin Cummins engines giving a total of 2,500 hp, were supplied to SRT between 1995 and 1996. They are GE model CM22-7i. 9 December 2015.

The Hitachi DMU forming train 439, the 11.45 Kaeng Khoi to Bua Yai, heads across the Pasak Jolasid Reservoir, near Khok Salung, on the direct line from Kaeng Khoi to Nong Khai. Note the unusual colour scheme which was applied to a few of these units by Nakhon Ratchasima depot. 16 November 2015.

Davenport No. 520 shunts DMUs at Nakhon Ratchasima depot. The depot maintains the Hitachi DMUs that operate in the area. A number of other Davenports are stored at the depot. Nakhon Ratchasima is 237 km from Bangkok on the North Eastern Line. 11 November 2015.

Hitachi No. 4509 shunts train 142, the 17.35 to Bangkok, into the platform at Ubon Ratchathani. This station is one of the termini of the North Eastern Line, 575 km from Bangkok. 23 June 2018.

The other terminus of the North Eastern Line was previously Nong Khai, 621 km from Bangkok. In 2009, the line was extended 5 km to Tha Na Laeng in Laos. Here, a Hitachi DMU, forming an international train from Nong Khai to Tha Na Laeng, is pictured crossing the Friendship Bridge over the Mekong River. The river forms the border between Thailand and Laos. 30 March 2015.

Japanese Pacifics Nos 850 and 824 run round a special train from Bangkok at Chachoengsao, on the occasion of the former King's birthday. Chachoengsao, 61 km from Bangkok on the Eastern Line, is the junction of the lines to Aranyaprathet, near the Cambodian border, and Ban Phu Ta Luang. 5 December 2015.

A Tokyu DMU forming train 280, the 06.40 Aranyaprathet to Bangkok, arrives at the small station of Bang Nam Prieo, north of Chachoengsao. 13 December 2015.

A freight-only line, running from Khlong Sip Kao Junction to Kaeng Khoi, diverges from the Eastern Line 25 km north of Chachoengsao. Here, Alsthom No. 4147, with a barrier wagon behind the locomotive, heads south with a train of LPG tanks for Bang Lamung, while General Electric GEA No. 4536 waits in the loop at Ongkharak with a northbound oil train. 18 April 2015.

Newly delivered Qishuyan SDA3 locomotives stand at the purpose-built maintenance facility at Sri Racha, on the line to Ban Phu Ta Luang. The locomotives are, from left to right, Nos 5106, 5107, 5110 and 5109. These locomotives have now taken over most of the freight workings in the area, including the container trains to Laem Chabang Port and the oil tank trains serving the Esso refinery at Laem Chabang. 2 May 2015.

Before the Qishuyan SDA3 locomotives took over these workings, Hitachi No. 4511 approaches the entrance to Laem Chabang Port with a container train from Lat Krabang. The Esso refinery is behind the train. 4 May 2015.

Hitachi No. 4516 approaches Taling Chan Junction station, west of Bangkok, with train 37, the 15.10 Bangkok to Su-ngai Kolok on the Malaysian border. Taling Chan is the junction of the Southern Line and the line to Thonburi, seen in the foreground. Thailand has been investing heavily in its transport infrastructure, evidence of which can be seen here. 17 December 2017.

The remaining section of the old Burma Railway diverges from the Southern Line at Nong Pladuk Junction, 64 km from Thonburi, and runs for 130 km to Nam Tok, its present day terminus. The history of this railway, constructed by the Japanese using forced labour during the Second World War, has been well documented elsewhere. During its journeys between Bangkok and Singapore, the Eastern and Oriental Express luxury train pays regular visits to the old Burma Railway. Here, the train has arrived at Kanchanaburi behind GE No. 4037, after a visit to the River Kwai Bridge. 15 March 2018.

From late November until early December each year, a festival, featuring a son et lumière, is held at the River Kwai Bridge. One attraction of the evening shows is a steam-hauled freight train crossing the bridge, hauled by one of the two Japanese 2-6-0 locomotives pictured here at Kanchanaburi. On the left is No. 713, with its Japanese number on its smokebox. No. 715 is on the right. Both were built by Hitachi in 1935. 27 November 2015.

GE No. 4037 sets out across the famous River Kwai Bridge, near Kanchanaburi, with train 258, the 12.55 Nam Tok to Thonburi. Note the tourists standing in one of the refuges on the bridge. These GEs are the usual motive power on this line, although Alsthoms may appear on trains 257 and 258. 17 March 2018.

GE No. 4018 heads train 257, the 07.45 Thonburi to Nam Tok, past fields of sugar cane and corn, between Wang Lan and Na Kan. Banana plants can also be seen growing in the valley. 20 November 2015.

Viewed from the restaurant of the River Kwai Cabin Resort, GE No. 4018 crosses the Wang Pho Viaduct with train 258, the 12.55 Nam Tok to Thonburi. 20 November 2015.

GE No. 4045 approaches Tham Krasae Bridge station at the eastern end of the Wang Pho Viaduct with train 258, the 12.55 Nam Tok to Thonburi. 26 February 2016.

GE No. 4036 approaches the 323 road crossing, south of Ban Pu Pong, with train 486, the 15.30 Nam Tok to Nong Pladuk Junction. The locomotive is in the revised livery applied to many of the class in recent years. 1 March 2019.

Ratchaburi is 117 km from Bangkok on the Southern Line. Permanent way tractor No. 4 waits in the loop with a short train of rails for train 43, the 08.05 Bangkok to Surat Thani, to cross. 23 April 2014.

Henschel diesel-hydraulic No. 75 shunts a permanent way train, with its train engine GE No. 4039 still attached, at Chumpon, 485 km south of Bangkok. 8 April 2008.

Henschel No. 3015 shunts extra coaches on to train 174, the 13.00 Nakhon Si Thammarat to Bangkok, at Surat Thani, 651 km from Bangkok. Henschel supplied twenty-seven of these B-B diesel-hydraulics to SRT between 1963 and 1964. They were fitted with Maybach/Mercedes engines of 1,200 hp. This locomotive was the last operational member of the class at this time, although there were also a few rebuilt locomotives used by the Italian-Thai Company on infrastructure work. 18 January 2009.

GEA No. 4555 departs from Nakhon Si Thammarat with train 86, the 15.00 to Bangkok. In the background, GE No. 4048 waits for departure time with a local train to Phattalung. Nakhon Si Thammarat is located at the end of a branch off the Southern Line, 832 km from Bangkok. Train 86 is scheduled to arrive at Bangkok at 05.10 the following day. 9 December 2009.

Krupp diesel-hydraulic No. 3115 shunts a guard's van at Hat Yai Junction. Hat Yai is located 945 km from Bangkok and 45 km from Padang Besar, on the Malaysian border. Trains from Bangkok to Su-ngai Kolok have coaches added and removed here, while the through train that ran to Butterworth in Malaysia now terminates here. This was one of the last centres of regular steam operation in Thailand. 22 December 2004.

Around 67 km long, the Maeklong Railway consists of two sections, separated by the Tha Chin River. The first section runs from Wong Wian Wai station, in the west of Bangkok, to Maha Chai station at Samut Sakhon. Tokyu DMUs operate all trains on both sections of the railway. Here, a Tokyu DMU stands outside the maintenance facility behind Maha Chai station. A market surrounds the station. 28 April 2014.

A ferry across the Tha Chin River connects Maha Chai and Ban Laem stations. The second section of the Maeklong Railway runs from Ban Laem station to Maeklong station at Samut Songkhram. Market traders display their wares on the railway line at Maeklong station. The goods are removed when a train is due and quickly replaced after the train has passed. Here, a Tokyu DMU, forming train 4382, the 10.20 to Ban Laem, heads away from Maeklong station. 30 March 2014.

Myanmar

Dalian Bo-Bo-Bo diesel-electric DF.2062 departs from Yangon Central station with train 31, the 08.00 to Naypyitaw. Two Kawasaki diesel-hydraulic shunters, with DD.521 at the front, are on the left. Yangon, formerly known as Rangoon, is Myanmar's largest city, and the former capital. The previous Yangon Central station was destroyed in 1943, the present-day station being completed in 1954. 14 February 2018.

Plinthed at Yangon Central station is this A class 4-6-4T, built by Beyer, Peacock & Company in 1916, works number 5923. This locomotive, one of a batch of eight, was operational until around 2004. 14 February 2018.

YDM4 Co-Co diesel-electric DF.1336 departs from Yangon Central with train 89, the 07.15 to Mawlamyine (also known as Moulmein). One of the station pilots, Kawasaki DD.522, is on the left. Diesel locomotives in Myanmar are numbered as follows. D stands for diesel. The number of axles is represented by the second letter, A for one, B for two, etc. The first one or two digits give the approximate power of the locomotive and the last two are the locomotive number. So, DF.1336 is a six-axle diesel of around 1,300 hp, while DD.522 is a four-axle diesel of around 500 hp. 25 November 2018.

Dalian DF.2048 eases out of Yangon Central with train 61, the 16.00 to Bagan, around 700 km north of Yangon in the Mandalay region. The locomotive, type CKD7B, has three two-axle bogies instead of the more usual two three-axle arrangement, so the wheel arrangement is Bo-Bo-Bo or tri-Bo. This is to accommodate Myanmar's tight curves and steep gradients. This wheel arrangement was also used on earlier Alsthom locomotives in Myanmar. 25 November 2018.

Alsthom Bo-Bo-Bo diesel-electric DF.1622 of 1974 approaches Yangon Central with an anticlockwise circle line train. This line runs around Yangon and is an interesting experience, taking around three and a half hours and giving passengers the opportunity to see something of local life. Many of these Alsthom locomotives have been fitted with Chinese A8V190ZL engines, from Jinan diesel engine company, rated at around 1,200 hp. One of the platforms of Pagoda Road station can be seen in the background. 28 November 2018.

Some of the crew of Alsthom Bo-Bo diesel-electric DD.933 of 1977 stand on the front of the locomotive as it heads a northbound suburban train away from Yangon Central. A number of these locomotives, built around 1975, have been fitted with Caterpillar 3512 marine engines of 860 hp, replacing the original MGO V12ASHR engines of 900 hp. The carriage sidings, with a Kawasaki shunter, are in the background. 22 February 2018.

Alsthom Bo-Bo-Bo diesel-electric DF.1263 approaches Pazundaung, one station east of Yangon Central, with a northbound suburban train. This locomotive, built using components from accident-damaged locomotives of the same type, carries a 'Myanma Railways Insein Locomotive Workshop 1993' plate. 14 February 2018.

A heavily loaded, former Japanese Railways, DMU departs from Mahlwagon station with an anticlockwise circle line train. Note the JR and Japanese writing on the destination blind. Underneath it says 'Kururi Line' in English, a line operated by the East Japan Railway Company. In 2005, a number of Japanese railway companies donated various older DMUs to Myanmar Railways. They are used on local trains around Yangon, as well as on longer distance services in other parts of the country. 16 February 2018.

A DMU, made up of ex-Japanese Railways (JR Central) KiHa 11 single-unit cars, pauses at Mahlwagon station with a northbound suburban train. Sixteen of these units were supplied to Myanmar in 2015. A large freight yard and Myanmar's main diesel depot are close to Mahlwagon station, around 2 km east of Yangon Central. 15 February 2018.

Alsthom Bo-Bo-Bo diesel-electric DF.1631 of 1978 pauses at Thingangyun station with a southbound local train to Yangon. This locomotive has been fitted with an A8V190ZL eight-cylinder marine engine, built by the Jinan Diesel Engine Co. Ltd, China. The coaches used on suburban trains have wooden seats and open windows. 22 February 2018.

Alsthom Bo-Bo-Bo diesel-electric DF.1221 arrives at Toegyaunggalay with the 10.45 local train from Dagon University to Yangon. Toegyaunggalay, on the main line towards Bago and the north, is the junction for the suburban lines to Dagon University, Eastern University and Thilawa. 25 November 2018.

The last station served by suburban trains, on the main line to Bago and the north, is Ywathagyi, around 13 km from Yangon Central and 5.5 km north of Toegyaunggalay. Here, Alsthom DF.1250, looking smart in a fresh coat of paint, is pictured approaching Ywathagyi station with a northbound freight. The train originated at Mahlwagon freight yard. 25 November 2018.

The 12.25 from Yangon to Thilawa, hauled by DD.932, has stopped short of Thilawa station and the locomotive has run round the train. Alsthom DF.1246, with a van behind the locomotive, is running on to the train, ready to draw it into the platform. This procedure was carried out because the points at the far end of the loop in the station were blocked by wagons. Thilawa is at the end of a branch line from Toegyaunggalay. 13 November 2018.

Alsthom DF.1255 of 1984 arrives at Kyeemyindine station, north-west of Yangon Central, with an anticlockwise circle line train. Semaphore signals still control the loops. This locomotive was assembled at Insein Works. Originally fitted with a SACM MGO12VBSHR of 1,200 hp, it has been re-engined with a Jinan A8V190ZL engine. 16 February 2018.

YDM4 DF.1333 pauses at Thein Zeik with train 89, the 07.15 Yangon to Mawlamyine. Thein Zeik is 127 km from Yangon. The locomotive is a refurbished ex-Indian Railways YDM4 supplied through Rail India Technical & Economic Services Ltd (RITES). The work was carried out in India at the Golden Rock Railway Workshop in Ponmalai, Tiruchirappalli. 15 November 2018.

Alsthom DF.1228, built in 1964, runs light engine through Mawlamyine station. This Mawlamyine station, 182 km from Yangon, is a new station, opened in 2006, after the completion of the Thanlwin River Bridge connected the railway from Yangon to the section from Mawlamyine to Dawei. Previously, passengers had to cross the Thanlwin River by ferry. Mawlamyine is the capital of Mon State. 16 November 2018.

YDM4 DF.1339 departs from Bago with train 90, the 08.00 Mawlamyine to Yangon. Bago, on the Yangon to Mandalay line, is the junction of the line to Mawlamyine and Dawei. Bago railway station retains two signal boxes and a fine selection of semaphore signals, making it an interesting centre for the railway enthusiast. However, the line is being modernised and the old signalling will soon be replaced. 21 November 2018.

Alsthom DF.1235, built in 1969, heads a mixed freight, bound for Yangon, out of the yard at Bago and past the mechanical signal box at the south end of the station. 19 November 2018.

Alsthom DF.1229 waits in the yard at Bago with a southbound freight. The locomotive, built in 1968, was fitted with a MGO12VBSHR from SACM, France. The engine has since been replaced with a Jinan A8V190ZL engine. 19 February 2018.

Bago locomotive depot is home to the few remaining operational steam locomotives in Myanmar, which are used on occasional special trains. Here, YD 2-8-2 No. 964 rests in the shed at Bago. The YD class was built for both India and Burma. This locomotive is one of twenty built by Vulcan Foundry for Burma between 1948 and 1949, works number 5728. 18 February 2018.

Alsthom DF.1205 shunts at Bago. It is one of six hood unit locomotives, fitted with MGO16VHSR engines of 1200 hp, built for Myanmar in 1957. Later Alsthom locomotives, built with full width bodies, were developments of this successful class. Note the goat lying in the foreground, undisturbed by the railway action. 19 February 2018.

A fine old signal gantry stands near the signal box at the south end of Bago station. Note that the spectacles have been removed from the signals. Japanese railcar RBE.2516, on permanent way duty, is about to pass under the gantry as it heads towards Yangon. RBE stands for Rail Bus Engine. 2 March 2019.

YDM4 DF.1336 is about to pass under the signal gantry at the north end of Bago station, as it arrives with train 90, the 08.00 Mawlamyine to Yangon. Note the washing put out to dry on the ground between the tracks. The YDM4 type, ALCo export locomotive model DL535, was widely used on the Indian metre gauge, with around 800 built in total. Some locomotives were built by the American Locomotive Company (ALCo) and the Montreal Locomotive Works (MLW), but most were built at the Diesel Locomotive Works (DLW), Varanasi, India. 22 November 2018.

In the 1990s, around eighty railcars were built for use on local services. They were based on truck chassis and were often unique, built from whatever materials were available. They usually pulled trailers or coaches. Here, LRBE (Light Rail Bus Engine) No. 36 is standing outside Bago locomotive depot ready for its next working. With the arrival of DMUs from Japan, these LRBEs have largely disappeared. 13 February 2006. (Photo courtesy of James Waite)

YD 2-8-2 No. 972, Vulcan Foundry works number 5736 of 1949, rests between shunting duties close to Bago depot, while the crew take a break with some colleagues. The locomotive was overhauled at Insein Works in 2005, hence the smart appearance. 13 February 2006. (Photo courtesy of James Waite)

Pyuntaza, north of Bago on the Yangon to Mandalay line, still retains two signal boxes and a variety of semaphore signalling. Dalian Bo-Bo-Bo diesel-electric DF.2026 gets a green flag from the north signal box as it arrives at Pyuntaza with train 142/10, the previous day's 08.00 Shwenyaung to Yangon. The train is due to arrive at Yangon at 14.40. The locomotive was built in 1993 and is fitted with a Caterpillar 3516DI-TA engine producing around 2,000 hp. 20 November 2018.

Dalian DF.2049 passes the big bracket signal at the south end of Pyuntaza, as it departs from the station with train 32, the 08.00 Naypyitaw to Yangon. This 2,000 hp locomotive was built in 2008. 4 March 2019.

In 2019, nine steam locomotives were stored, inside and outside the shed, at Pyuntaza locomotive depot. Among the locomotives that were standing outside were 2-8-2 YD446, left, and 4-6-2 YB508. YD446 was built by SLM Winterthur for the Indian Railways *c.* 1928. Mixed traffic locomotive YB508, built by Vulcan Foundry, Newton-le-Willows, in 1947, was delivered direct to Rangoon. 4 March 2019.

Taungoo is situated 190 km north of Yangon on the line to Mandalay. Dalian DF.2091 starts away from the Taungoo station stop with train 12, the 06.00 Mandalay to Yangon, a journey of fifteen hours. Locomotives of this class are now being assembled, in co-operation with CRRC Dalian, at a recently completed locomotive factory in Naypyitaw. 26 February 2019.

A northbound oil tank train starts away from a brief stop at Taungoo station. Alsthom DF.1254 was assembled at Insein Locomotive Workshop in 1984, from parts supplied by Alsthom. The old water tower and the signal box, behind the footbridge, are on the left. 27 February 2019.

Dalian DF.2041 waits at Pyinmana before heading north with a train of rails. The locomotive was built in 1998 and is fitted with an MTU16V396TC14 engine of around 2,000 hp. Pyinmana signal box is behind the train. 24 February 2019.

Dalian DF.2096 arrives at Pyinmana with train 12, the 06.00 Mandalay to Yangon. This locomotive was one of the first to be assembled at Naypyitaw, using parts imported from CRRC Dalian, China. Pyinmana is 362 km from Yangon. 23 February 2019.

Japanese railcar RBE.2569 departs from Pyinmana with a short working to Tatkon, 28 km to the north. Built in 1985, it arrived in Myanmar in 2011, and is one of the many Japanese railcars and DMUs that are used in Myanmar. 24 February 2019.

Station pilot Alsthom DF.1237, built in 1968, shunts coaching stock at Naypyitaw. Naypyitaw, the present capital of Myanmar, was built on a site to the north of Pyinmana. Construction was completed by 2012. The station, built to serve the new capital, is also the site of the headquarters of Myanmar Railways. A small railway museum is located there. 23 February 2019.

Plinthed in Naypyitaw railway station is 2-4-0T A 01 (612 of 1873) built by Dübs & Company, Glasgow, for India. It entered service in Burma on 1 May 1877, according to information in the railway museum at Naypyitaw station, and is said to be the first steam locomotive to run in Burma. 22 February 2019.

In green livery and with an extension on its chimney, YB class Pacific No. 534 of 1947 is displayed on a short length of track, in front of Naypyitaw station. Fifty of these mixed traffic locomotives were built at the Vulcan Foundry, Newton-le-Willows, for Myanmar, and were shipped to Rangoon in 1947. 22 February 2019.

Eighteen new 1,350 hp Co-Co diesel-electric locomotives, built by DLW, Varanasi, India, were delivered to Myanmar Railways in 2018. The locomotives resemble the YDM4s but are designed for Myanmar's railways. They have updated cabs, AC-DC transmission, microprocessor controls, and are said to be very fuel efficient. Here, DF.1363 heads a Mandalay to Yangon freight train away from Naypyitaw. 24 February 2019.

Krupp B-B diesel-hydraulic DD.1217 of 1986 shunts wagons off a mixed train that has arrived at Myo Haung station from the south. The station is adjacent to the freight yard, 8 km south of Mandalay. Sifang Co-Co diesel-electric DF.1267 of 1995 is on the front of the train. The Krupp locomotive is fitted with an MTU 12V396TC13 engine of 1,200 hp. 2 December 2018.

Krupp DD.1217 shunts at Myo Haung yard, south of Mandalay. On the right, ALCo YDM4 DF.1345, imported from India in 2010, is stabled with a single van. 3 December 2018.

Krupp B-B diesel-hydraulic DD.945, model M1200BB, stands in Myo Haung freight yard between shunting duties. Twenty-seven of these locomotives, DD943 to DD969, were built for Myanmar Railways between 1978 and 1987. This locomotive was fitted with an MTU MA6V396T12 engine initially, later upgraded to a 12V396TC12. 2 December 2018.

One of the Indian-built diesel-electrics delivered in 2018, DF.1370, makes a fine sight as it departs from Mandalay with train 55, the 16.00 to Myitkyina, a journey of more than nineteen hours. Mandalay, a former capital, is the second largest city in Myanmar. It is 622 km north of Yangon by rail. 1 December 2018.

YDM4 DF.1361, fitted with an ALCo 251-D engine, departs from Mandalay with the 08.30 mixed train to Yangon. At the time of this photograph, it was the highest numbered, rebuilt YDM4 of the sixty-one in Myanmar. It had previously worked in Tanzania. 3 December 2018.

B-B diesel-hydraulic DD.1204 runs to the locomotive depot, after arriving at Mandalay with a passenger working. Built by Kisha Seizo Kaisha of Japan, it is fitted with a 1,200 hp MAN engine. Five other locomotives of this class of ten were re-engined with MTU 12V396TC12 engines. Other members of the class were stored in the depot. 1 December 2018.

Krupp B-B diesel-hydraulic DD.901 runs past the railway market as it arrives at Thu Ye Zae station in the north of Mandalay, with the 09.50 from Madaya. Once a station on the line that circled Mandalay, after a section was closed, it became the terminus of the line round the city, as well as the line to Madaya. The two lines divide at Oh Bo, 2 km to the north. 6 December 2018.

Krupp DD.901 waits to depart from Madaya with the 16.15 to Thu Ye Zae. The train will then travel round the city back to Mandalay, before returning the next day. Madaya is 15 km from Thu Ye Zae, at the end of a rural branch line. The locomotive is one of six 900 hp locomotives, model M800BB, delivered in 1969. They are fitted with MTU MA12V362 engines. 5 December 2019.

Malaysia

The West Coast Line of Malaysian Railways (Keretapi Tanah Melayu Berhad or KTM) runs from Padang Besar, on the Thailand border, through Malaysia to Singapore. The line is now double-tracked and electrified at 25 kV AC between Padang Besar and Butterworth, and on to the South. Before electrification, train 35, the 14.45 special express from Bangkok to Hat Yai, with two through coaches to Butterworth, departs from Arau on the West Coast Line with YDM4 No. 6543 in charge. Note the point signals on the left. 7 March 2010.

YDM4 No. 6685 runs into the loop at Arau with a southbound container train. The YDM4 Co-Co diesel-electric locomotives, ALCo export model DL535A, were built between 1961 and 1990 for the Indian metre gauge railways. The Y is for metre gauge, D for diesel, and M for mixed traffic. Around thirty of these locomotives were leased to KTM (Malaysian Railways) from 1996. 6 March 2010.

From 2005, twenty Co-Co diesel-electric locomotives, model CKD8E, were supplied to KTM by the Dalian Locomotive & Rolling Stock Company, China. They are fitted with MAN 16RK215T engines of 3,500 hp. Here, No. 29102 *Meranti* enters the loop at Gurun with a northbound container train. Gurun station is located on the West Coast Line between Su-ngai Petani and Alor Setar, north of Butterworth. 6 March 2010.

Seventeen Co-Co diesel-electric locomotives of classes 25/1 and 25/2 were built by General Motors (GM), Canada, in 1990 (25/1) and 1998 (25/2), model GT18LC-2. They were fitted with GM 8-645-E3C engines of 1,500 hp. Here, GM No. 25103 *Pulau Bidong* arrives at Su-ngai Petani with train 36, the international train from Butterworth to Hat Yai and Bangkok in Thailand. 13 April 2009.

GM diesel-electric No. 25112 *Pulau Tioman* stands at Bukit Mertajam with a train of cement tanks. Bukit Mertajam is the junction of the West Coast Line and the branch to Butterworth. The line is now electrified and the station has been rebuilt. 10 April 2009.

Bombardier Co-Co diesel-electric No. 26101 *Tanjung Aru* heads away from Bukit Mertajam, past a pair of bracket signals, with a container train from Butterworth to the north. From 2003, twenty of these 3,400-hp locomotives were supplied to KTM by Bombardier, Germany. Called Blue Tigers after the prototype, they are used on passenger trains as well as heavy freight. 11 April 2009.

Former Indian Railways' YDM4 diesel-electrics stand outside the shed at Butterworth locomotive depot. On the left is No. 6181, with No. 6685 on the right. The locomotives retain their Indian Railways' numbers. 5 March 2010.

Running long hood first, GM No. 25204 *Mutiara* approaches Butterworth station with a train of container flats from the container terminal. A Star Cruises ship, moored at the International Cruise Terminal, Penang, is in the background. 5 March 2010.

Hitachi No. 23101 *Amanah* departs from Butterworth with train 36, the 14.00 international train to Bangkok. The two SRT coaches will be attached to the main portion of the train at Hat Yai, Thailand, for the overnight journey to Bangkok. Butterworth is linked to Penang island by both ferries and a road bridge. 29 January 2008.

Plinthed at Butterworth station is English Electric 0-6-0 shunter No. 151.101. Built at the Vulcan Foundry, twenty of these diesel-electric locomotives were supplied to Malaya in 1948. The class was withdrawn between 1984 and 1991. 29 January 2008.

Kisha Seizo Kaisha of Japan supplied fifteen 400-hp diesel-hydraulic shunters to the Malaysian railways in 1964. By 2010, some of the locomotives were in use with contractors and No. 17105 (Barclay Mowlem 005) and No. 17103 (Barclay Mowlem 006) are pictured stored in the yard at Saphli, north of Chumpon, Thailand. 20 June 2010.

Toshiba No. 24104 *Mat Salleh* departs from Taiping, 96 km south of Butterworth, with train 4, the 09.10 Kuala Lumpur Sentral to Butterworth. This Taiping station, now preserved, was replaced by a new station to the north-east when the line was electrified. 12 April 2009.

Dalian No. 29120 *Kledang* is about to join the West Coast Line as it heads a train of cement tanks down the branch from the YTL cement works at Padang Rengas. 11 March 2010.

Bombardier No. 26116 *Tanjung Selatai* heads south at Padang Rengas with a train of cement tanks from the YTL cement works. 10 March 2010.

Dalian No. 29113 *Nyatoh* heads a southbound cement train, from the YTL works at Padang Rengas, through Kuala Kangsar. The station is 120 km south of Butterworth, on the West Coast Line. The formation for the new electrified railway is behind the fence on the right. 9 March 2010.

In 1983, Hitachi of Japan built fifteen Co-Co diesel-electric locomotives for KTM for use on front-line duties. They were fitted with Pielstick SP12 PA4V 200 VG engines of 2,160 hp. No. 23111 *Maju* is pictured running light engine through Ipoh. Ipoh, the northern limit of electrified services in 2010, is 206 km north of Kuala Lumpur. 2 July 2008.

In 1987, Toshiba of Japan built twenty-six Co-Co diesel-electric locomotives for KTM, fitted with Pielstick SP16 PA4V 200 VG engines of 2,400 hp. Here, Toshiba No. 24101 *Panglima Teja* heads the 08.00 Singapore to Butterworth through Kepong station, a KTM commuter station in northern Kuala Lumpur. The station was rebuilt and electrified in 1995. 6 February 2011.

A Class 91 electric multiple unit (EMU), forming the 13.45 Ipoh to Kuala Lumpur Sentral, heads through Kepong, as a Class 82 EMU departs with a northbound suburban service. Light engine No. 26106 *Tanjung Jara* waits at the red signal for the local train to clear the section. Built by Rotem and Mitsubishi Electric in 2009, the Class 91s were KTM's first EMUs designed for use on long-distance passenger trains. 6 February 2011.

Class 82 EMU No. 45 approaches Kepong with a suburban train to Seremban. Twenty-two of these three-car sets were built for KTM by the Union Carriage & Wagon Co. Ltd of South Africa between 1996 and 1997. All were withdrawn by 2015 because of the lack of availability of spares after the closure of the company. 3 February 2009.

Class 82 EMU No. 57 pauses at Sentul station, around 3 km from Kuala Lumpur Sentral. Hitachi No. 23115 *Setia* and an unidentified Class 26 stand in the locomotive depot at Sentul Works, next to the station. Previously the main railway works in Malaysia, the works itself was already closed by the time of this photograph, its operations moving to Batu Gajah, Perak. 1 February 2008.

Brush 0-6-0 diesel-hydraulic shunter No. 18110 stands outside the locomotive shed at Sentul Works, next to Sentul station. This is one of ten 650-hp locomotives purchased in 1978. One is now preserved at Johor Baru. A Class 24 is behind. 27 November 2002.

From 1971, English Electric built forty Co-Co diesel-electric locomotives for the Malaysian Railways. They were fitted with English Electric 8CSVT Mk 3 engines of 1,760 hp. All these locomotives are now withdrawn from service, but four have been preserved. One of the last of the class to be overhauled was No. 22115 *Kuala Lipis*, pictured here in Sentul Works. 27 November 2002.

This locomotive, No. 27101, was a prototype Co-Co diesel-electric built in India at DLW, Varanasi. However, no sales were obtained in Malaysia, KTM purchasing locomotives from China instead. Later, renumbered 6800, the locomotive was returned to India and is believed to have been sold to Mozambique. Here, the locomotive is pictured receiving attention at Sentul Works. 27 November 2002.

In 1983, Hitachi supplied ten 650-hp Bo-Bo diesel-electric locomotives to Malaysia, KTM numbers 19101 to 19110. Here, No. 19109 shunts the yard at Jalan Kastan, on the line from Kuala Lumpur to Port Klang. A freight line to the container terminal at North Port diverges from the main line here. 15 July 2010.

Because of a shortage of serviceable EMUs during 2010, some rush hour commuter trains were made up of units with generator wagons, hauled by diesel locomotives. Here, Toshiba No. 24107 *Raja Mahadi* is stabled at Jalan Kastan with an electric unit in between the morning and evening rush hours. No. 25107 *Pulau Langkawi* is on the other end of the train. 15 July 2010.

English Electric No. 22101 *Shah Alam* stands at the front of a line of withdrawn locomotives in the yard at Jalan Kastan. Behind are No. 22135 *Geliga*, No. 22125 *Telok Chempedak*, No. 22118 *Nilam Puri*, and No. 24106 *Long Jaffar*. The locomotives had been moved to Jalan Kastan as a result of the closure of Sentul Works. 3 February 2009.

Pacific No. 564.36 *Temerloh*, built in 1946, is displayed at Gemas. It is one of forty locomotives built by the North British Locomotive Works, Glasgow, and is the last steam locomotive to have worked on KTM. Officially preserved in 1975, it occasionally worked in the 1980s and the early 1990s. It has since been moved to a new railway museum in the old station at Johor Bahru. 28 January 2009.

The East Coast Line, also known as the Jungle Line, runs between Gemas, the junction with the West Coast Line, and Tumpat in Kelantan. Toshiba No. 24110 *Hang Lekir* arrives at Tumpat with train 14, the previous day's 18.00 Singapore to Tumpat. Tumpat is 528 km from Gemas and 750 km from Singapore. 23 June 2008.

After arriving with train 16, the previous day's 20.30 from Kuala Lumpur Sentral, YDM4 No. 6675 is turned on the manually operated turntable at Tumpat, ready for its next working south. Both the Class 25 and the YDM4 hood units normally run with their short hood leading. Tumpat, the terminus of the East Coast Line, has carriage sidings, a small locomotive shed, and servicing facilities for locomotives and rolling stock. 23 June 2008.

English Electric Co-Co diesel-electric No. 22127 *Tanjong Bunga* runs out of the locomotive shed into the sunshine at Tumpat. The locomotive was one of the last of the class to remain in service and was kept at Tumpat as a standby at this time. Occasional permanent way duties were also undertaken. 22 January 2009.

YDM4 No. 6635 departs from Pasir Mas with train 16, the 20.30 Kuala Lumpur Sentral to Tumpat. Pasir Mas, 25 km from Tumpat, was the junction where the now disused international line to Su-ngai Kolok in Thailand left the East Coast Line from Gemas to Tumpat. 22 January 2009.

GM No. 25112 *Pulau Tioman* is pictured during a lengthy stop at Tanah Merah, 53 km south of Tumpat on the Jungle Line, with train 94, the 13.50 Gua Musang to Tumpat. A mail coach is behind the locomotive. 27 June 2008.

The crew of No. 6635 take the token for the single track, as train 91, the 06.15 Tumpat to Kuala Lipis, arrives at Padang Tunku. The station is near Kuala Lipis, where the train is due to arrive at 13.15. It is scheduled to stop there until 15.00, when it will continue to Gemas as train 93. Note the signal on the platform with an arm for each direction, a common feature of stations on the Jungle Line. 26 January 2009.

Bombardier No. 26111 *Tanjung Piai* heads north from Johor Bahru with train 62, the 08.30 Singapore to Kluang in Malaysia, a distance of 113 km. Johor Bahru is situated at the end of the causeway from Singapore Island. The 3,400 hp of the locomotive should be more than adequate for the two coaches and generator van! 19 April 2009.

Bombardier No. 26107 *Tanjung Karang* approaches the old station at Johor Bahru with train 6, the 14.00 Singapore to Kuala Lumpur. A KTM shuttle service from Johor Bahru to Singapore now runs from Johor Bahru Sentral, built next to the old station, over the causeway to Woodlands Train Checkpoint. Long-distance trains no longer run from Singapore Island. 15 April 2009.

Hitachi No. 19110 shunts the yard and carriage sidings at Singapore. Container flats and vans stand in the yard, and Singapore railway station can be seen in the right background. 24 November 2002.

Toshiba No. 24120 *Seri Lanang* shunts the stock of train 6, the 15.05 to Kuala Lumpur, into Singapore station, also known as Tanjong Pagar or Keppel Road station. Ownership of the railway land, which had previously belonged to KTM, reverted to Singapore after the line closed in 2011. 24 November 2002.

YDM4 No. 6657 waits to depart from Singapore station, the former southern terminus of KTM, with train 14, the 18.00 Singapore to Tumpat. The station closed on 30 June 2011, when passenger services were terminated at Woodlands, just across the causeway from Johor Bahru in Malaysia. The last train from Singapore station was driven by Sultan Ibrahim Ismail of Johor. The station is now a national monument. 17 April 2009.

The Sabah State Railway (SSR), on the island of Borneo, is a 134-km line from Tanjung Aru to Tenom. Railcar No. 3102 is heading south, about 3 km south of Tanjung Aru, alongside the main motorway from Kota Kinabalu. The railcar is Wickham number 10513 of 1971, one of six built that year for the SSR. The bodies were supplied by British Rail Engineering at Litchurch Lane, Derby. 17 May 2006. (Photo courtesy of James Waite)

Vulcan Foundry 2-6-2 No. 60.016 of 1955 arrives at Tanjung Aru with a return SSR public excursion. The locomotive is based on a series of YD class 2-8-2s, previously built for Burma, and was the last steam locomotive to be built by Vulcan Foundry. The leading coach, used as a kitchen car, is an ex-diesel railcar, one of several built by Wickham of Ware between the mid-1950s and 1971. This station has now been swept away by the construction of a shopping mall and a road/rail interchange. 17 May 2006. (Photo courtesy of James Waite)

Vietnam

Plinthed at Saigon station, the southern terminus of the 1,600-km main line of Vietnam Railways (Duong sat Viet Nam or DSVN) from Hanoi, is 2-8-2 No. 141.158. This ZL class locomotive was one of sixty-seven locomotives built by Tanshang Works, China, between 1965 and 1974, based on earlier locomotives supplied by Société Alsacienne de Construction Mécaniques (SACM), France. 13 March 2019.

GE Bo-Bo diesel-electric D9E.248, on station pilot duties, waits to cross Tran Van Dang between Saigon locomotive depot and carriage sidings and the railway station. Forty-seven of these locomotives, GE model U8B, were supplied to Vietnam Railways in the early 1960s, fitted with Caterpillar D379 engines producing 910 hp. A few locomotives have been fitted with more powerful engines and have been reclassified as D10E. 12 March 2019.

GE Bo-Bo diesel-electric D9E.254 shunts the carriage sidings at Saigon (Ho Chi Minh City), while Ziyang D19E.917 runs on to the locomotive depot, on the right. 29 November 2019.

The two different versions of the metre-gauge D19E Co-Co diesel-electrics are pictured together at Hanoi locomotive depot. Later version D19E.947 is on the left, with earlier version D19E.926 on the right. A total of eighty locomotives were built by CSR Ziyang, China, and the Gia Lam Workshops in Vietnam. 28 March 2008. (Photo courtesy of James Waite)

Ziyang D19E.913 crosses Pham Van Dong as it leads train SE6, the 09.15 Saigon to Hanoi, out of Saigon. This locomotive is one of the first forty with the square body shape. These Co-Co diesel-electric locomotives, CSR Ziyang model CKD7F, are fitted with Caterpillar CAT3512B engines producing 1,950 hp. 30 November 2019.

Co-Co diesel-electric D19E.966 heads train SE10, the 14.40 to Hanoi, away from Saigon. This locomotive is one of the last forty locomotives, built with a more rounded body shape. These second series locomotives were also built by CSR Ziyang and the Gia Lam Workshops, Vietnam. 19 March 2019.

ALCo YDM4 D13E.708 departs from Phan Thiet with train SPT1, the 13.05 Phan Thiet to Saigon. Phan Thiet is a fishing port and coastal resort about 200 km north of Saigon, located at the end of a short branch line from Binh Tuan on the Saigon to Hanoi main line. Twenty-five of these locomotives, with Alco 251D-6 engines of 1,350 hp, were supplied to Vietnam by DLW from around 1984. They are similar to the ones in Malaysia and Myanmar, but with higher cab roofs. 15 March 2019.

B-B diesel-hydraulics D11H.348 and D11H.356 stand outside Da Nang locomotive depot. Built by the 23rd August Works, Bucharest, Romania, fifty-eight of these locomotives were supplied to Vietnam Railways between 1978 and 1980. They are model LD-110-M-VN2 and are fitted with Maybach MB 820 DC engines of 1,100 hp. Many of these locomotives are now withdrawn. 3 January 2006.

Diesel-hydraulic D11H.357 approaches Da Nang with train SE21, the 06.25 Hue to Saigon. Da Nang station is a terminus, where trains using the Hanoi to Saigon main line reverse. A D19E class locomotive will take the train on to Saigon. 23 November 2019.

Co-Co diesel-electric D20E.011 heads away from Da Nang with a single container. Sixteen of these locomotives were built for DSVN by Siemens AG, Germany, between 2006 and 2007. They are model AR15 VR Asia Runner, fitted with an MTU 12V 4000R41 engine of 2,010 hp. Note the loop line in the road on the right, originally built to turn steam locomotives. 23 November 2019.

The loop line at Da Nang, built to turn steam locomotives, sees little use today since most of the diesel fleet operating around Da Nang have cabs at each end. The D18E class is a single cab design, however, and D18E.602 is pictured running round the loop towards the carriage and wagon facility. The locomotive is one of sixteen 1,800 hp Co-Co diesel-electrics built by Cockerill, Belgium, in 1983. 21 November 2019.

Shunter D2M rests between its duties at the carriage and wagon facility, located opposite the locomotive depot at Da Nang. This locomotive was rebuilt from a D4H diesel-hydraulic into a diesel-mechanical shunter. It is powered by a Kamaz truck engine. 22 November 2019.

Bo-Bo diesel-electric D12E.643 departs from Gia Lam, across the Red River from Hanoi and Long Bien, with train LP3, the 09.28 Long Bien to Haiphong. Forty of these general purpose 1,200-hp locomotives, model DEV-736, were supplied by Ceskomoravska-Kolben-Danek (CKD), Prague, Czechoslovakia, between 1985 and 1990. 4 November 2019.

CKD D12E.630 crosses Dien Bien Phu after emerging from one of the narrow streets between Long Bien and Hanoi station. The train is LP2, the 06.10 Haiphong to Hanoi. To avoid road traffic delays, daytime trains only run over this section of line at weekends. At other times they run to and from Long Bien station. 3 November 2019.

Diesel-electric D12E.643 trails at the rear of train LP2, the 06.10 Haiphong to Long Bien, as it crosses Long Bien Bridge over the Red River. D12E.655 is on the front of the train. The train will wait at Long Bien station until 09.28, when it will depart as train LP3 to Haiphong. D12E.655 will be detached at Gia Lam. The 2.4-km cantilever bridge was opened in 1903. 15 November 2019.

CKD diesel-electric D12E.643 is pictured in one of the narrow streets in Haiphong, soon after leaving the railway station and crossing Cau Dat with train LP8, the 15.00 Haiphong to Hanoi. Since it is a weekend, the train will run through to Hanoi instead of terminating at Long Bien. 9 November 2019.

Diesel-hydraulics D4H.862, left, D4H.458, and a third, unidentified, member of the class stand at Hanoi locomotive depot. These B-B locomotives, type TU7, were built by Kambarka Engineering Works, in the USSR, from the mid-1970s. 247 of the export version, TU7E, were supplied to Vietnam around 1985. Fitted with V12 ID12-400 engines of 400 hp, they were used on a wide variety of services including shunting and local passenger trains. Many of these locomotives have been withdrawn but D4H.488 was seen at work at Haiphong in November 2019 and two members of the class are still in use on the railway at Da Lat. 28 March 2008. (Photo courtesy of James Waite)

A rack and adhesion railway ran from the Saigon to Hanoi main line at Thap Cham for 84 km to the city of Da Lat, located 1,500 metres above sea level on the Langbian Plateau. Construction of the railway commenced in 1908 with regular operations ending during the Vietnam War. In the 1990s, the 7-km section from Da Lat to Trai Mat was reopened as a tourist attraction. Here, D4H.866 is pictured heading away from Da Lat with the 09.50 to Trai Mat. 28 November 2019.

A small number of standard gauge D4H locomotives, class D4HR, were used on the lines in the north. Here, D4HR.864 is pictured standing at Luu Xa station with a permanent way train, on the mixed gauge railway south of Thai Nguyen. 31 March 2008. (Photo courtesy of James Waite)

Former Queensland Railways' DH class B-B diesel-hydraulic, D5H.055, is pictured at Yen Bai station during a pause in its station pilot and yard activities. This class was built between 1968 and 1970 by Walkers Ltd, Maryborough, Queensland, Australia, model GH500. Thirteen, delivered between 1993 and 1995, were converted from 3 feet 6 inches to metre gauge. They are fitted with six-cylinder Caterpillar D355E diesel engines of 465 hp and are class D5H in Vietnam. 17 November 2019.

An unidentified Chinese DFH21 class B-B diesel-hydraulic stands at Yen Bai locomotive depot. Thirty of these locomotives were purchased second-hand from China in 2006. Built by Sifang, China, in 1977, they are fitted with V12 180ZJA engines of 1,000 hp. In Vietnam, they are class D10H. Two D5H class locomotives, D5H.055 and D5H.054, are on the left. 28 March 2008. (Photo courtesy of James Waite)

Diesel-hydraulic D10H.029 is turned on the wye at Yen Bai locomotive depot. These locomotives handle most of the freight traffic on the line to Lao Cai. 16 November 2019.

One of two diesel-electric power cars built in Vietnam in 2002, D8E.1001 is pictured in Hanoi locomotive depot, minus its nose. It is believed that these locomotives were to be used in the same way as the InterCity 125 power cars in Great Britain, but were actually used on ordinary passenger trains. They were fitted with V12 Caterpillar CAT3412E engines producing 871 hp. They had a maximum speed of 120 kph. 1 April 2008. (Photo courtesy of James Waite)

In the north of Vietnam, there are several sections of standard gauge and mixed gauge track, including a line from Gia Lam to China. A daily passenger train also runs on the standard gauge line from Yen Vien station, near Hanoi, to Halong. Many locals travel on this train to sell their produce at a market on Halong station. Here, Qishuyan D14E.2011 approaches Halong with two coaches forming train 51501, the 04.55 Yen Vien to Halong. 13 November 2019.

Standard gauge Co-Co diesel-electric D14E.2013 runs round its train, the 04.55 from Yen Vien, at Halong station. This locomotive, model JMD 1360, is one of five built for DSVN by CSR Qishuyan in 2002. It is fitted with a Caterpillar 3508B engine producing 1,300 hp. The locomotive is running on dual gauge track, but this did not extend beyond the station area towards Hanoi at the time of this photograph. Note the semaphore signal in the background. 10 November 2019.

Cambodia

Société Franco-Belge at Raismes, France built 2-6-2 131.106 in 1912. This locomotive is pictured plinthed at Phnom Penh station, Cambodia. The station building is visible in the background. Various other steam locomotives still survived in derelict condition at Phnom Penh locomotive depot at this time. 28 February 2018.

In 2014, PTG tours arranged a photo charter from Phnom Penh to Takeo Ra, with Pacific 231.501. The locomotive had recently been overhauled, and was the only working steam locomotive in Cambodia at the time. It is pictured here in the western outskirts of Phnom Penh. This locomotive class was built by Société Alsacienne de Constructions Mécaniques (SACM) at Graffenstaden and Haine-Saint-Pierre between 1939 and 1948. 26 March 2014. (Photo courtesy of James Waite)

Standing in the yard at Phnom Penh depot are two Pacifics in derelict condition. The number 231.507 is visible on the buffer beam of the locomotive at the front. Previously it had 231.506 painted over it, but this has disappeared after years of outdoor storage. The locomotive behind is believed to be No. 231.509. While the identity of these and other Pacifics stored inside the shed is not clear, at least some of them previously worked in Vietnam. 3 December 2019.

Two Alsthom AD12B Bo-Bo diesel-electric locomotives stand outside the locomotive shed at Phnom Penh. BB1053, on the left, is the double cab version, and BB.1001 is the single cab type. The two types were delivered between 1968 and 1969. 0-4-0 shunter Bde.406 can just be seen on the right. 11 April 2006.

Alsthom Bo-Bo diesel-electric BB.1055 departs from Phnom Penh with the Sundays-only 16.00 to Sihanoukville. The locomotive is one of six 1,200-hp locomotives supplied by Alsthom in 1969. It is model AD12B (double cab). Note the old water crane on the right. 11 March 2018.

Alsthom Bo-Bo diesel-electric locomotives BB.1005, left, and BB1004 stand at Phnom Penh locomotive depot. These are two of six single cab locomotives supplied by Alsthom to Cambodia in 1968 and 1969. They are model AD12B (single cab) and are fitted with engines of 1,200 hp. CKD BB.1010, in blue livery, is behind BB1004. 3 September 2006.

Seven 450 hp 0-4-0 diesel-electric shunting locomotives were supplied to Cambodia by Établissements Fauvet Girel and Compagnie Électro-Mécanique (CEM) of France in 1966. These were numbered Bde.401 to Bde.407. Here, Bde.406 stands outside the locomotive depot at Phnom Penh. An old wheelset stands on the track behind the locomotive. 3 September 2006.

In 1994, CKD of Prague supplied two 415-hp 0-4-0 diesel-electric shunting locomotives to Cambodia, model T234, Nos Bde.410 and Bde.411. As well as shunting, these locomotives are also used on both passenger and freight trains. Here, Bde.410 is pictured between shunting duties at Phnom Penh. Phnom Penh station, built in 1932 during the French colonial era, is visible in the background. 10 April 2006.

Disused DMU ZZ.803, built by Waggonfabrik Uerdingen in 1969, stands at Phnom Penh locomotive depot. CKD shunter Bde.410 is alongside. 27 March 2008. (Photo courtesy of James Waite)

An overhauled DMU, made up of ZZ.802 and ZZ.803, heads away from Phnom Penh station, past the locomotive depot, with the 16.00 Phnom Penh to Sihanoukville. Note the van, used to transport motor bikes, at the rear of the train. 1 December 2019.

Bo-Bo diesel-electrics BB.1011 of 1991 and BB.1013 of 1993 stand outside the locomotive shed at Phnom Penh. These 987-hp locomotives were built by CKD and are model DEV-736. They are similar to the Vietnam D12E class. Pacific 231.501 is in the background. 27 March 2008. (Photo courtesy of James Waite)

ALCo No. 6546 has just crossed the Hanoi-Phnom Penh Friendship Boulevard as it heads away from Phnom Penh with the 16.00 to Sihanoukville. The train is made up of diesel units and a van. The locomotive, painted in the latest Royal Railway livery, is one of the YDM4s that previously worked in Malaysia. Ten of these locomotives arrived in Cambodia in 2019. 15 December 2019.

Railcar AS1002 approaches Phnom Penh Airport station with the 09.30 working from Phnom Penh. The station is at the end of a 1.6-km street section which branches off the Sihanoukville line. Three of these railcars were built in Mexico in 2018 for the Royal Railway. They are currently used on services to the airport and Sihanoukville. 1 December 2019.

ALCo No. 6633 waits in the loop at Takeo station, with a container train to Sihanoukville, for the railcar forming the 07.00 service to Sihanoukville to pass. Takeo is the first stop for trains from Phnom Penh to Sihanoukville, two hours after leaving Phnom Penh. 6 December 2019.

CKD Bo-Bo diesel-electric BB.1012 waits at Kampot, 166 km from Phnom Penh, while passengers' motorbikes are unloaded from the van at the front of the train. On this occasion, the train is formed of four diesel units, serving as coaches. The train is the 07.00 Phnom Penh to Sihanoukville. Passenger services ran on Fridays to Mondays at this time. 3 March 2018.

Passengers wait at Kampot station as railcar AS1001 arrives. The train is the 07.00 Sihanoukville to Phnom Penh. Kampot, two hours from Sihanoukville and four and a half hours from Phnom Penh, is the second of the two intermediate stations between Phnom Penh and Sihanoukville. 14 December 2019.

Sihanoukville, 267 km from Phnom Penh, is the terminus of the Southern Line. After arriving at Sihanoukville with the 07.00 from Phnom Penh, BB.1012 has been uncoupled and is ready to shunt its train. The train includes a car transporter at the back for passengers' cars, which will be unloaded from the adjacent platform. 3 March 2018.

CSR Qishuyan Bo-Bo diesel-electric BB.1061 stands at Sihanoukville station. One of two locomotives, model CKD6B, supplied by Qishuyan in 2004, it is fitted with a Caterpillar 3508B engine of 1,100 hp. Bde.411 and Bde.410 are behind, having brought a freight from Phnom Penh. The locomotives have been repainted into the orange livery applied during Toll Holdings involvement with the railway. 3 March 2018.

When, after fourteen years with no scheduled passenger trains, services to Sihanoukville recommenced in May 2016, Royal Railway Cambodia used the Uerdingen DMUs as passenger stock, hauled by a diesel locomotive. Here, before being returned to full working order, the DMUs which formed the passenger stock of the 07.00 from Phnom Penh are shunted by BB.1055 at Sihanoukville. 4 March 2018.

Alsthom BB.1055 shunts its train at Sihanoukville after arriving with the 07.00 from Phnom Penh. The van behind the locomotive is used for the transport of motorbikes, while the passengers' cars that were transported on the train have already been unloaded from the flat wagons on the left. 4 March 2018.